Good Living Skills
Learned from my Mother

Good Living Skills
Learned from my Mother

Cathy Burnham Martin

Quiet Thunder Publishing
Manchester, NH   Columbus, NC   Naples, FL

www.QTPublishing.com

This title and more are also featured at
www.GoodLiving123.com

Good Living Skills
Learned from my Mother

Copyright © 2020 Quiet Thunder Publishing
Manchester, NH   Columbus, NC   Naples, FL

Paperback edition: ISBN 978-1-939220-51-6
eBook edition: ISBN 978-1-939220-52-3
Audiobook edition: ISBN 978-1-939220-53-0

Published and printed in the United States of America.

Library of Congress Control Number:
2020910856

Dedication

I am deeply honored and mightily blessed to be able to dedicate this book to my mother, Glenna Burnham, as we celebrate her 90th birthday, June 25, 2020. Mom remains smiling, vibrant, and active, a survivor of challenges and loss, and a beacon of light for anyone who needs help putting one foot in front of the other on any day. For ninety years my mother, has been in the process of becoming… of growing… of evolving.

Through it all she has shared without limits, worked with ceaseless energy, and taught by shining example. She has been my Encourager Extraordinaire, my #1 cheerleader, and the long-standing president of my "fan club."

Happiest Birthday wishes, Mom! Thank you for giving to us the most precious gift possible… YOU, being the most perfectly wonderful mother you truly are.

Foreword

The art of mothering
is to teach the art of living to children.
-- Dr. Elaine Heffner (1927 -)
American psychotherapist, parent educator & lecturer

Good living skills aren't simply "born" in any of us. They are taught... repeatedly. They are engrained in our practices... persistently. They are emblazoned on our minds... steadfastly. We learn them through example, through teaching, and through experience.

When we are blessed with a wonderful mother, we are forever touched by someone more than just special. Mothers are both catalyst and glue for our families. They teach, and they build our foundations. They listen, and they pick us back up. They celebrate, and they console. A mother's love and devotion know no bounds.

As children, we may not often recognize their work as not only valuable, but vital to our development into powerfully positive people. As adults we more clearly see how precious they are and how essential their endeavors remain.

Some of us lose our mothers far too early in Life. Some of us enjoy the precious gift of a mother's long and active Life. Some of us must grow up without a mother. When lucky, someone else, perhaps a sister or an aunt, a grandparent, brother, father, or dear friend, may help fill the gaps.

If you were not blessed with the time and love that a mother brings, let this book warm and enliven your heart, like loving arms securely hugging you. If you have enjoyed the blessings of a loving Mother, pay it forward by employing the good living skills she taught and exemplified.

We all need to stay in the learning mode for our entire lives. Whether we learned any of these skills as youngsters or we are still learning them now, being well-equipped to enjoy good living gives us great positive power.

Thanks to 20:20 hindsight, *Good Living Skills Learned from My Mother* helps us reflect on how some of their precious wisdom makes our lives far better. This book salutes and celebrates the gifts that a mother's teachings can be.

Table of Contents
Page Skill

Page Skill

Page **Skill**

Skill 1
<u>Say Something Nice or Say Nothing at All</u>

My mother taught me to be nice to everybody.
And she said something before I left home.
She said, 'I want you to always remember that the
person you are in this world
is a reflection of the job I did as a mother.'
-- Jason Segel (1980 -)
American actor, comedian & screenwriter

If our mothers only taught us one thing, this just might be it. This lesson goes beyond politeness. It rings with respect.

We all know people who seem to have no filters in their communication. While we may, initially at least, appreciate their frankness, especially when they say things that we may be thinking, we also recognize that they might have had far more positive impact had they used some thoughtful consideration before spewing.

It may feel refreshing in many aspects to speak "nastiness." It may even feel earned or justified. It may simply be accidental.

However, our negativity can also be hurtful, regardless of deliberate intent. This applies not only to *what* we say, but *how* we say it.

It takes no greater effort to say something pleasant than to say something distasteful. None of us can un-ring the bell. So, we are best to not speak out of negative emotion.

I have friends who follow the "say 3 nice things" rule. This means that if they've said something negative to or about the other person, they then must follow-up by sharing 3 positive things about that person.

So, as usual, Mom was right. She taught me to look for the positive in every person and situation, even on those darkest days.

> ***It may be possible to gild pure gold,***
> ***but who can make his mother more beautiful?***
> -- Mahatma Gandhi (1869 – 1948)
> Indian lawyer, anti-colonial nationalist & political ethicist

Skill 2
Turn That Frown Upside Down

As my mom always said, 'You'd rather have smile lines than frown lines.'
-- Cindy Crawford (1966 -)
American model & actress

Likely, we've all heard that it takes less muscles to smile than to frown. I guess this is one area where we do not need to focus on building strength and fitness to frown more readily. Let's try to just keep smiling.

If Life hasn't smacked you up the side of the head yet, it will. Many bumps, bruises, and pitfalls lie in our paths. Heartache, pain, and loss are unfortunate parts of each of our worlds.

All in all, it's not easy living in this place called Life. But we can make it worthwhile.

But, as Mom taught me, Life is just too short to spend it frowning. If I am having a bad day, it is not my right to bring someone else down with me.

She is most likely the inspiration for my developing my goal to live with contagious enthusiasm. That evolved into the central theme, that resonates on my website, GoodLiving123.com.

Think of the many "lines" you may have heard that reflect the reality that our time is very short on this planet. Life isn't a rehearsal. There's no hitting rewind. Time flies.

Life is too short to:
- be anything but happy.
- to wake up with regrets.
- to wait.
- to drink bad coffee or cheap wine.
- to do things you don't love doing.

- to worry about stupid things.

- to argue and fight.

- to be little or to belittle.

- to let small-minded people mess with your head… or heart.

- not to live it up a little.

- to waste.

We all "get it" that Life brings no guarantees of happiness. But if we can learn to turn our frown upside down on the tough days, just imagine how much happier we can be the rest of the time, too!

If I have done anything in life worth attention,
I feel sure that I inherited the disposition
from my mother.
-- Booker T. Washington (1856 – 1915)
American educator, author & orator

Skill 3
Make Your Bed Daily

There is no influence so powerful as that of the mother.
-- Sara Josepha Hale (1788 – 1879)
American writer & editor;
author of "Mary Had a Little Lamb"

"You can make your bed with a smile, or you can make your bed with a frown, but you're going to make your bed." Those are words I heard often from my all-time Great American Mother, Glenna Burnham. She had her hands full with my crummy childhood attitude, but a mere child was no match for this strong, determined woman! Sure, she insisted on having a clean house, but she wanted happy, healthy children even more. My mother's multitude of lessons, once learned, would make me a far happier, healthier, and more resilient adult.

Medical experts agree that having a positive attitude means getting sick less often and, if sick, being able to recover quickly. Great attitudes are not easy to come by.

What's even more annoying is the simple fact that we can't blame a bad attitude on genetics. We can't control what happens to us or around us, but we have complete control over how we respond to it. That response can have an amazing impact on our health, both immediately and collectively.

Think about people with the uncanny ability to roll with the punches. Challenges seem to roll off their backs like water off a duck. Paddling like crazy underneath the water's surface could mean stomachs twisted into knots or increased risk of heart disease because of inner stress.

When impersonating Fernando Lamas, comedian Billy Crystal said, "*It's better to look good than to feel good, and you look mahhhvelous.*" But that was comedy; this is real life. We need to feel good in order to look good, and it all starts with how we think. As I expounded upon in my book *Healthy Thinking Habits: Seven Attitude Skills Simplified*, healthy eating habits get plenty of attention.

However, healthy *thinking* habits should too. That deals with our attitude.

We often hear that success is determined much more by attitude than aptitude or skill. Even noted genius Albert Einstein said, "*Imagination is more important than information.*" I call that a ringing endorsement of the idea that attitude beats aptitude.

Generating a great attitude is no small task; it's an ongoing process for the rest of our happy lives. Thanks, Mom, yet again. You glowed with positive attitude, even when the chips were down.

She taught us to not dwell on whatever negative might be swirling about us. When we dwell on negative, we give it more power than need be.

When I must deal with something very negative, I try not to procrastinate about it. Mom taught me that, too. Just get the worst over with first.

I liken that to Nicholas Chamfort's perspective, "Swallow a toad in the morning and you will likely encounter nothing more disgusting the rest of the day." Charming food for thought. (Very "punny," I know.)

Motherhood is the biggest gamble in the world.
It is the glorious life force.
It's huge and scary – it's an act of infinite optimism.
-- Gilda Radner (1946 – 1989)
American comedienne

Skill 4
Do It Right

> *My mom is a hard worker.*
> *She puts her head down and she gets it done.*
> *And she finds a way to have fun.*
> *She always says, 'Happiness is your own responsibility.'*
> *That's probably what I quote from her*
> *and live by the most.*
> -- Jennifer Garner (1972 -)
> American actress & entrepreneur

We have all heard that if we're going to do something, we should do it right the first time. Unfortunately, that is not always possible.

Regardless, Mom taught us that if we were going to do anything, we should try to do it right, or keep trying until we could. Sometimes this takes training. Sometimes it takes patience. Sometimes it takes experience. Sometimes it takes all that and more.

When she was first teaching my sister and I how to cook, hindsight reminds me that we were not really cooking at the beginning. Mom would let us play with the scraps from her pie crust dough. We could cut shapes and sprinkle them with sugar, raisins, or cinnamon before she popped them into the oven to bake.

Then she graduated us to turning the scraps into the most delightful treat. We'd roll out the scraps of dough into one sheet. Next, we brushed it with melted butter and sprinkled it with raisins and cinnamon-sugar. Finally, we rolled it all up like a skinny jellyroll, before baking. A slice of that toasty treat encouraged us to want to cook more.

She wasn't going to make it all easy for us. Mom wanted us to learn real skills.

It seemed very tedious at times. However, I am thankful for these skills every day.

I recall that learning to cream butter and peanut butter together for peanut butter cookies seemed to take endless hours and more strength than my skinny little child arms could stand. Our mother was relentless. She would not take over the task.

"Keep trying," she would firmly say. We learned to do it right. Mom didn't earn a "Best Cook in Town" moniker lightly.

There is no way to be a perfect mother,
and a million ways to be a good one.
-- Jill Churchill (1943 -)
American author

Skill 5
Turn "What Could Have Been" into "What Is"

Acceptance, tolerance, bravery, compassion.
These are the things my mom taught me.
-- Stefani Joanne Angelina Germanotta "Lady Gaga" (1986 -)
American singer, songwriter & actress

We all know people who don't live up to their potential. This is disappointing at the very least and utterly sad regardless. If we can help it, we never want to leave potential undeveloped.

"You are better than that," I can hear Mom saying. She always challenged us to do our best and be our best.

Whatever our talents may be, we do best when we actively work with them. Now, that doesn't mean that our circumstances can or can't make developing our talents more or less challenging.

For example, what if we have music or other artistic talent, but your family doesn't have the money to afford lessons or special schooling? We can still develop our potential by tapping into free resources and local opportunities. These may present themselves at church, school, or other community events.

What's important is to try.
Give it our best. Stretch. Reach.

We never want to look back with regrets over something we didn't try. We want to strive to look at our lives with satisfaction at any age.

It's very grounding to be able to look at our life and smile. We may not have reached the tippy top in any field or activity. But if we gave it our best, we will never feel our time and efforts were wasted.

We are better than that. We can and should live with no regrets.

Motherhood: All love begins and ends there.
-- Robert Browning (1812 – 1889)
English poet & playwright

Skill 6
Count to 10

Be the parent today
you want your kids to remember tomorrow.
-- Unknown

Mom is a champion counter. I likely helped her achieve this, although unintentionally. Instead of losing her patience with me when I was being a particularly challenging child, Mom would count, "1, 2, 3, 4, 5, 6, 7, 8, 9, 10." Okay. I knew I had badly annoyed her.

In fact, sometimes she would repeat the 1-10 counting... several times if need be. Sometimes she'd count slowly. Sometimes very rapidly. Mom was a creative counter.

The good living skill here is learning not to overreact. When we quickly react to some negative stimulus, we tend to react and become negative ourselves.

Counting to ten can help us develop patience. It buys us a few moments to pause and think more rationally.

So much of our lives seem to be filled with rushing, zooming, and always being in a hurry. We don't like to wait for anything. I call it "microwave mentality." When microwave ovens first came out, I remember marveling at the speed and ease of warming something up. Wow! We could cook a baked potato in minutes instead of an hour.

However, not too much later, we grew impatient and forget how impressed we had been with the little oven's speed. So, we watch the microwave oven's digital timer counting down. But microwave mentality means we tend to not wait for the bell to ring. We stop it early. We are in a hurry. Thus, I love the "Count to 10" good living skill. Patience serves us well in all aspects of life.

Patience, persistence and perspiration
make an unbeatable combination for success.
-- Napoleon Hill (1883 – 1970)
American author

Skill 7
Put Your Best Foot Forward

Your child will follow your example, not your advice.
-- Unknown

Mom taught us to always put our best foot forward. Often this just meant we should be polite and respectful to people. Other times it reflected her strong sense of decency as it applied to how we dressed.

For example, I was not permitted to wear cut-off jeans in public. When we went to Church, we wore our Sunday best clothes, never something casual. That would have seemed disrespectful. She didn't care one wit about how other people dressed.

We might whine, "But Mom! Everybody else is doing this or that!" Our protests fell on deaf ears. She was teaching us.

As an adult, I got a funny reminder of this good living skill. We had joined some friends for a Key West, Florida, celebration called "Fantasy Fest." It was Halloween, and there were some amazingly creative costumes, some of which were eye-brow-raising in their skimpiness.

Well, it was Key West after all. Then we saw it, as we walked down Duval Street to a restaurant for lunch. A particularly rotund man was walking just ahead of us, sporting nothing more than a G-string. Yup. I had found my new mantra.

Just because you can, doesn't mean you should.

We laughed. We repeated my mantra. We laughed some more.

Okay, that is an extreme example, but we do learn from the examples set for us at very early ages.

That's likely why I owned 3-inch high-heeled pumps in every color when I entered my working years. Mom always wore pumps. My mini skirt hems dropped to below the knee. This is how a lady dressed. I learned.

It takes no extra effort to put our best foot forward, so why not? Our lives are enhanced whenever we learn and display good manners.

A mother is clothed with strength and dignity,
laughs without fear of the future.
When she speaks her words are wise
and she gives instructions with kindness.
The Bible. Proverbs 31:25-26

Skill 8
Be Kind

It is not how much we do,
but how much love we put in the doing.
It is not how much we give,
but how much love we put in the giving.
-- Mother Teresa (1910 – 1997)
Albanian-Indian Roman Catholic Nun

We have likely all seen various posters advocating the practice of "random acts of kindness." These things make us smile. Hopefully, they also remind us to do just that.

Kindness never hurt anyone. In fact, acts of kindness can do great good, especially if someone is a little lonely or feeling down. Something we do not readily do, however, is to apply our kindness efforts to *ourselves*. We may well know that we should be kind to others, but we are not often as equally kind to ourselves. And why not?

We are just as deserving of our kindness as everyone else.

Good living means taking care not to put ourselves down. It is far too easy to think or talk negatively about ourselves. We lack self-confidence. So, Mom wouldn't let us talk unkindly about ourselves or anyone else.

Kindness costs nothing. There is no excuse for not being kind. If we fail to be kind, we likely fail at other important skills, too.

Teaching us the importance of being kind, also meant Mom was teaching us to share. As three siblings, we could certainly squabble with the best of them. She stood steadfastly by, encouraging us to do better.

If she said it once, she said it a hundred times. "You can do this." Teaching us to encourage others, as well as ourselves, was also teaching us to be kind.

Mom was an advocate of kindness. She also advocated skills like fairness and sharing. A great example of this shines through Mom's handling of the traditional rift over the last piece of pie in the pan.

If two people wanted it, she let one cut it in half and the other select their half first. If all three of us wanted it, one cuts it, the second one selects first, and the third gets to have it in the actual pie plate with all the other yummy crumbs and juices.

We'd draw straws to see if we were the cutter or selector. She didn't invent this approach, but she taught us well by applying it.

A mother is a person who,
seeing there are only four pieces of pie for five people,
promptly announces she never did care for pie.
-- Robert Quillen (1887 – 1948)
American journalist & humorist

Skill 9
Work Comes Before Play

The phrase 'working mother' is redundant.
-- Jane Sellman (1987 -)
American writer and writing consultant

Never can I recall my mother not working. Whether she was working around the house or working at Dad's office or working on some Church or civic event, she was *always* working.

Work was a natural part of life. My folks had learned and exuded good work ethic. Mom saw to it that we learned to have a good work ethic, too.

So, the answer was, "Yes, you can go over to Susan's house to play. But first, you need to do x-y-z tasks." There were house cleaning chores. And it seemed that there were endless flower beds or rows of vegetables that needed weeding.

None of it hurt us one bit. In fact, I am proud of my folks for instilling a strong work ethic in us all.

Play is important. We never want to lose our fun spirit of play. However, it's easier to enjoy our play time when we have already accomplished things from that Need to Do List. Thanks, Mom!

If evolution really works,
how come mothers only have two hands?
-- Milton Berle (1908 – 2002)
American comedian & actor

Skill 10
If You Start Something, Finish It

Words are meaningless
without intent and follow through.
-- Zig Ziglar (1926 – 2012)
American author & motivational speaker

Sometimes we take on too much, be it too much work or too many projects. We get too many sticks in the fire, so to speak.

My Mom's twin sister dubbed me the Queen of Unfinished Projects. She gave me a cute little pillow to remind me. No wonder I always called this aunt my "Other Mother." The good living skill learned here is to not take on so much that we can't finish things.

I recall working on homemade Christmas gifts right up to the moment I needed to wrap them so folks could unwrap them. Sometimes they were finished. Other times, I had to confiscate the gift and finish it.

Ah, timing. I realize that we all have the same 24 hours each and every day. Time management remained a challenge for me well into my young adult years.

Finally, I learned that my lack of organization impacted others. I needed to organize my chaos. I like to pull my own weight. Group projects helped me get my act together. If you're like me, we must continually work on not taking on too much.

I feel rather akin to the comic character, Ado Annie, in the musical "Oklahoma!" She sings the song, "I'm Just a Girl Who Can't Say No." Though the circumstances are different, the result rings true. I struggled mightily with saying, "No." I just didn't ever want to let someone else down. What I struggled with was the fact that in taking on too much, I was a greater risk of letting someone down. I also was a risk of letting myself down or, at the very least, placing unnecessary amounts of stress on myself.

So, as we strengthen our ability to prioritize, we can more readily succeed at finishing any project we undertake. Being known as someone who takes commitments seriously is important. We've **got** this!

Individual commitment to a group effort –
that is what makes a team work, a company work,
a society work, a civilization work.
-- Vince Lombardi (1913 – 1970)
American football coach & NFL executive

Skill 11
Value Property, but Not Above People

She is far more precious than jewels.
The Bible   Proverbs 3:15

This good living skill is about respect. I believe we all know that we should love people and use things, never the other way around.

However, Mom taught me that I needed to learn to take care of my things, our possessions. Whatever it is, it may well be the only one we'll get.

When I was 10 years old, I got a fast first lesson in this. I'd been given my very first wristwatch. I was thrilled. A genuine Timex watch. I was so excited, I hated to remove it.

Naturally, when I went to the YWCA for weekly swimming lessons, I had to remove the precious watch. Mom had suggested I leave it at home, but, oh, no. I had to wear it.

Well, you can probably guess what happened. It was all new to me. When I put my clothes back on and packed my swimsuit in my bag, I failed to see the watch on the shelf in my little locker room dressing stall. When I got to the car, Mom asked where my watch was. I desperately raced back inside, but the watch was already gone! No one ever turned it in, and I never forgot such a thing again.

My initial heartbreak helped teach me the good living skill to value my property. More than 10 years would pass before I could get another wristwatch. Now, when people remark at how well I take care of my possessions, I recall my first wristwatch. I had *not* taken such care.

So, I don't advocate valuing property more than people, EVER! This would only lead to heartache and unnecessary angst.

Do you recall that favorite aunt of mine… the one who dubbed me the queen of unfinished projects? She'd never married or had children.

Her twin sister, my Mom, says that this aunt had sort of adopted me, like the daughter she never had. I was doubly blessed to have a fabulous Mother, plus my Other Mother.

Well, this aunt, my Other Mother, added me to the deed to her house so it would automatically be mine upon her passing. That was very loving of her. She contended it was well-deserved since I was the only one of her 4 nieces and nephews to have maintained a strong relationship with her throughout our adult lives.

Plus, both my husband and I had given her much, both in the way of goods and work on her home, especially during her last 10-15 years. So, she saw this decision as earned, rather than a gift or inheritance.

Unfortunately, an evil, elder abuse con man came into her final year of life. We had to protect her assets in her Trust.

Sadly, after this dear aunt passed away, some among the other three of her 4 nieces and nephews did not like learning that this aunt had meant her home to be mine, rather than divided up four ways through the Trust.

Yup, it all came down to potential money some thought should go in their own pockets. Yikes! Such is life. I was glad that I had not loved her with the hope of "inheriting" something.

Isn't it funny (though in a twisted way) that people who have no interest nor involvement in someone's life for 40 years suddenly get a powerful fascination when they think there might be money for them through some inheritance. Though many people knew of my aunt's true intent, I chose to back off and not fight to hold what was rightfully mine. No way would I let "stuff" drive a wedge into my family.

Both my aunt's friends and my own pointed out that I was permitting them to take her old, but adorable home away from me. True, but I had learned this good living skill well.

I recognize that I got a genuine, priceless treasure that they all missed. I enjoyed several decades of being part of her life. No one can take that from me, and no house is worth more than that, even if it had been a multi-million-dollar mansion.

The worth of people is far greater than any of their things.

One other aspect of this good living skill that is worthy of note is to treat other people's property respectfully. Sometimes we may not see the value in the same light as they do. However, we are respecting the individual when we respect their property. We are utterly disrespecting people when we disrespect their property.

If people respect you, respect them back.
If people disrespect you, respect them back anyway.
They represent their ideology.
You represent yours.
-- Anonymous

Skill 12
Count Your Blessings

> *The heart that gives thanks is a happy one,*
> *for we cannot feel thankful and unhappy*
> *at the same time.*
> -- Douglas Wood (1951 -)
> American author and songwriter

Learning to appreciate whatever we may have is a bountiful good living skill. Mom taught this gem to us regularly. She taught us kids from an early age to always say, "Thank you."

It mattered not if what had been done, said, or given was large or small. We knew we should be grateful.

Now, I did not always "get" the lesson, I assure you. Children can be picky eaters, and I was no exception.

I know I was not the only child who often heard some variation of the expression, "Clean your plate. There are starving children in the world."

A real wise guy, I often retorted with some nasty quip, such as, "Okay. Send it to them."

My family did not have a lot of money. However, we always had plenty of food on our plates. I had absolutely zero concept of what it might be to truly go hungry… meal after meal after meal. I was blessed.

Perhaps this is one reason my folks always kept us involved in some Church activity to help those who were less fortunate. Whether it was caroling for shut-ins, making teddy bears for children in the orphanage, or secretly delivering half our Halloween candy pre-dawn the following morning to the porches of people who were truly poor, they kept us focused. I am so very grateful. I am constantly thankful.

Whatever our circumstances, many have less.

It's one thing to feel gratitude. It's another to express the gratitude we feel... often. I love the philosophy of living with an "attitude of gratitude."

When I first heard that expression around 1980, I simply thought it had nice ring to it. And yet, the meaning resounded with me. I couldn't get it out of my mind. Remember, I am always on the hunt to learn new and better ways to build a great attitude.

With an "attitude of gratitude," we have developed gratitude habits. We feel grateful. We say, "Thank you" often. We take actions that express our gratitude.

When we count our blessings, it shows. We smile more frequently. We stay healthier. Our friendships are deeper, even with those we may see infrequently. We're more productive, sleep better, and even handle stress more deftly.

Whether our blessings are large or small, we need to count them. We need to stay keenly aware of how fortunate we are for those blessings. If we are not grateful for our blessings, we might start taking them for granted. THAT would be a bad living skill, most assuredly.

Remember, we are not born with gratitude. We learn it. We learn to count our blessings, large and small. This helps us to appreciate each and every blessing. When we are particularly blessed, the "attitude of gratitude" is one of many good living skills learned from our mothers.

Everything I am, you helped me to be.
Unknown

Skill 13
Live Generously

*You will discover that you have two hands. One is for
helping yourself. The other is for helping others.*
-- Audrey Hepburn (1929 – 1993)
British actress & humanitarian

Giving generously is not just for famous philanthropists
with extremely deep pockets. We can all give. We give even
more when we live generously.

Naturally, we do not all have an identical financial
capacity for giving. Nor do we have identical inclinations to
give. While it's impressive when we learn of someone giving
tremendous amounts of their financial wealth to help others,
I am also struck by how many people who have the ability to
give, choose *not* to do so.

There is no requirement. There is no law requiring us to
give away money to someone or something we deem
deserving or worthy.

Both the act of giving and the act of *not* giving reflect on our character.

Setting money aside, we all do have the same capacity for giving of our time. We all get the same 24 hours each day. Naturally, we have different requirements that drain our time. We may work, have family responsibilities, be serving as caretakers, or have many other aspects of life that nibble away at our 24 hours.

What we do with whatever non-committed hours we may have is purely personal. Mom always stressed that helping others is important. She said that when you give, you actually **get** even more than you give.

She was right, naturally. We get satisfaction. We are humbled. We build our ability to empathize. We feel happy. We feel valuable and valued… worthy. We also get positive social connections.

Oh, and how great is it that giving is contagious?!? Giving encourages others to give. What a great way to live with contagious enthusiasm!

Don't ever feel "less" if you do not have the ability to give money. Money is a renewable resource. Time is not. Our time is even more valuable than money.

Give whatever *you* can give. And give as often as possible. It makes us better people.

By being yourself,
you put something wonderful in the world
that was not there before.
-- Edwin Elliot (1851 – 1937)
British mathematician

Skill 14
Compassion Counts

They may forget what you said,
but they will never forget how you made them feel.
-- Carl W. Buechner (1926 -)
Presbyterian minister

Whatever we may do, we should try to do it with genuinely positive feelings. If we have compassion as one of those feelings, it means we have honed the good living skill of being able to understand the feelings of others. We can relate to them.

Mom used to say, "There, but for the grace of God." She understood that someone else's struggle could have easily been her own or our own. Naturally, this meant that she taught us well to help anyone who was less fortunate.

Sometimes this help was in the form of giving, be it food, clothing, or service. The very best times were those when we could help others help themselves. That not only helped them immediately, but in the long run.

This makes me recall an expression. Give a man a fish, and you feed him for a day. Teach a man to fish, and you feed him for a lifetime. That says it all.

We need to help others help themselves.

When I hosted the Easter Seals telethon for more than a decade, my favorite expression was that donations were more than a handout... they provided a hand *up*. And the clients receiving those moneys worked hard for every single bit of gain they accomplished as they learned to walk or talk, or any number of other skills.

Of course, I advocate giving a handout when we can, but I promote giving a hand *up* always. These are the things we can do in our families, our schools, our communities, our churches, our jobs, or whatever may be our spheres of influence and activity.

Just imagine if more and more people truly behaved compassionately. Like positive ripples on the water's surface when a pebble is tossed in, the rings of compassion would keep expanding and intersecting with rings of compassion from miles and miles away. Compassion can make the world a very wonderful place indeed.

I am sure that if the mothers of various nations
could meet,
there would be no more wars.
-- E. M. Forster (1879 — 1970)
English novelist

Skill 15
Family First

To the world, you are a mother,
but to your family, you are the world.
-- Unknown

Dad ran his plumbing and heating company as if it was part of his family. In a way, it was. That business provided the roof over our heads and the food on our table.

On holidays, he'd give his workers the day off. He would make himself the "man on call" for anyone's emergency. Inevitably, this meant delays in our family's holiday dinners, as he would be out making sure some other family got their heat or water working again.

Meanwhile, Mom became an expert at preparing fabulous meals that could wait. Further, at the same time as she was preparing the meal for our gathering of various aunts, uncles, cousins, and grandparents, she also prepared a duplicate meal.

This was a meal we would take to feed some distant, elder relatives. She knew they would not be bothering to prepare anything special for themselves. So, we would feast. AND we would take another feast to serve to others.

Whether people were actual relatives or just close to our family became inseparable. We called various folks Aunt and Uncle, though they were not relatives by either blood or marriage.

We were taught to care for those close to our family as if they were truly family, because they were... just not by blood. These relationships provide a foundation of values. We benefit by having wonderful memories and traditions.

This is why we keep scrapbooks. It's fulfilling and fun to look back at pictures and keepsakes. Looking back at colorful pages filled with family, activities, and history brings us great joy, if we let it. And it can provide warm comfort in tough times.

So, Mom taught us to live our lives fully and cherish the beauty along the way. She also taught us to keep family first. All the other important "things" will keep.

A big part of this skill involves staying in touch. All that busy, busy, busy scheduling is frustrating. Worse, it separates us from those who truly matter. All too soon, loved ones will be gone along with the opportunities to connect.

There are friends, there is family,
and then there are friends that become family.
-- Unknown

Skill 16
Recognize Achievements

She drove me to ballet class...
and she took me to every audition.
She'd be proud of me if I was still sitting in that seat
or if I was watching from home.
She believes in me
and that's why this [award] is for her.
She's a wonderful mother.
-- Elisabeth Moss (1982 -)
American actress

While she served long and well as president of my (non-existent) fan club, Mom cheered me on, insisting that I could do anything I wanted if I set my mind to it. At the same time, she taught me to celebrate both the effort and success of *others*.

There could be no room for jealousy when you genuinely care. Sometimes we get the blue ribbon. Sometimes someone else does.

Mom also taught to not always seek credit, even when you've earned it. Doing the right things is not about being *recognized* for doing the right things. It's simply about *doing* the right things.

Anything is actually possible when we don't focus on who may or may not get credit for it. On the other hand, recognition is a great motivator. Applause can be far more motivating than money.

> **It is amazing what can be accomplished**
> **when nobody cares about who gets the credit.**
> -- Robert Yates (1943 — 2017)
> Nascar owner

As Mom said, "It doesn't matter if *any*one is given credit. It matters that the job gets done well." My spin on that was to give credit to others or to the team for successes and goals met or exceeded. Then I'd put the blame for whatever goes wrong on myself. That always worked well for me in business. It helped keep my head landing on my pillow comfortably at night.

Teamwork is the quintessential contradiction of a society grounded in individual achievement.
-- Marvin Weisbord (1931 -)
Author and management consultant

Skill 17
Stand for What Is Right

In matters of principle, stand like a rock;
in matters of taste, swim with the current.
-- Thomas Jefferson (1743 – 1826)
Diplomat, lawyer, and 3rd President of the United States

While I can be something of a character, being a person *of* good character is far more memorable. And, I believe, it is far more important.

Mom taught the good living skill lesson on this one also. She'd say, "Stand for something or you'll fall for anything."

She was very big on not caring if we were popular with the "in" crowd. She cared that we were doing what was right and building a strong, positive belief system.

Even if it seems to be unpopular, when you know in your heart what is right, she'd always encourage us to not fall to peer pressure. Plus, we had the further encouragement of not wanting to let our parents down.

Mom encouraged us to support those who support fairness.

As we all know, not everyone does. There always seem to be famous cheaters about or people who simply focus on how to seek or expand their own personal gain. Fairness rarely comes into play with them. Worse, these are often the same people who espouse ad nauseum about how important fairness is to them. Yeah, they want to be treated fairly, even though they may not treat others fairly.

In standing for what is right, we also need to learn to choose our battles carefully. Some arguments or battles are overly complicated, too difficult, or simply irrelevant. There is no need to waste energy on every little fray.

We could drive ourselves crazy if we tried to jump in and help in every single circumstance. Even if some battles we miss are important ones, we do not have the time nor personal resources to spread ourselves too thinly all the time.

We need time to rest and recover, to grow and strengthen. Only then are we better prepared for the next situation for which we may be needed.

Doing what's right is not always easy, but it is far easier in the long run than turning our backs on what's right. Facts are facts, even when we may not like believing them.

Mothers all want their sons to grow up to be president,
but they don't want them
to become politicians in the process.
-- John F. Kennedy (1917 – 1963)
35th President of the United States

Skill 18
Peaches and Cream

To describe my mother would be to write about a hurricane in its perfect power.
Or the climbing, falling colors of a rainbow.
-- Maya Angelou (Marguerite Annie Johnson) (1928 – 2014)
American writer, poet & civil rights activist

My mother is an absolutely priceless gem. And if gems are formed by years of intense pressure, then I assuredly helped polish my mom. (Sorry for being a brat, Mom!)

Mom knew that dealing with a challenging child created volatile scenarios. However, she never let her frustration with me overflow into other aspects of life. That ability to compartmentalize can be powerful.

Growing up, I remember my mother scolding me loudly over one troublesome thing or another that I'd done. The greatest talent displayed itself if the telephone rang in the midst of a vibrant scolding.

Her voice and tone shifted immediately to a melodic "peaches and cream," as though everything was just as smooth as could be. Mom figured the caller didn't need to know she was contending with a hyperactive brat.

I'd taunt her by singing out, "Peaches and cream!" And I'd stay just out of her reach to foil her attempts to grab me. In those days, she was constrained by a telephone cord.

Her lesson was clear. Her frustrations had been caused by me and had nothing to do with the caller. She could separate. It took me time to understand.

Initially, I just tossed it off, thinking it was insincere. I was far from right. Life doesn't always seem fair. Life *isn't* always fair.

Unfairness in Life does not mean we need to behave unfairly toward others.

We are all much happier when we refuse to let bitterness become the "flavor of the day" on any day. We live better when we don't allow something negative to flow into the rest of our life.

*Holding on to anger is like grasping a hot coal with the intent of throwing it at someone else;
you are the one who gets burned.*
-- Gautama Buddha (circa 480 BCE – circa 400 BCE)
Ancient Indian philosopher and spiritual leader

Skill 19
Become a Solid Foundation

My mother is my root, my foundation.
She planted the seed that I base my life on,
and that is the belief that the ability to achieve
starts in your mind.
-- Michael Jordan (1963 -)
Professional basketball player & NBA owner

We are not all blessed with a family situation that keeps us balanced or prepares us to be positive, productive adults. While I count my personal blessings from having a super family, I also recognize the need to share skills with everyone.

Someone just may need to hear the good words we say. They may need our encouragement to not give up. Reinforcement could make a huge difference in helping someone believe that where there's a will, there's a way.

When we build a solid foundation, we also enable ourselves to trust in ourselves and our intuition. Especially when we find ourselves in situations where it may appear that our personal skill set isn't valuable, we need to think again. I learned from Mom to ask myself, "What can I add? What might I do to make this go better?"

It reminds me of family ski outings as a child. We three children would ski down the trails over and over again. We would often spy Dad at a trail's edge. He wasn't a skier, but he would bring his snowshoes and traipse all over the mountain with us. Mom had no interest in snowshoeing or skiing. However, she found a perfect niche for her skills. Mom would select a picnic table in the lodge. When we came in for a break, she always had a cup of hot cocoa ready.

Plus, she'd thought ahead and packed a perfect lunch for everyone. She provided a solid foundation. We could count on that safe place to land.

She didn't do this sort of thing once. She made it a habit. She taught us by living her lessons out loud. She taught us to not give up, to be consistent, and to be persistent.

The truth of being persistent is that it works. It gets the job done. We only get flustered when we stop short of our goal. We plan and prepare for a particular project as a three-hour task. Perhaps it turns out to be a five-hour task. We can't win if we give up after four hours.

The adage is true that says, "A big shot is just a little shot that kept on shooting." Movie fans of the "Star Wars" films remember Yoda's sage remark, *"Do or do not. There is no try."*

So much has been written and said about being persistent and consistent. In all walks of life, it is seen as key to success, self-image, and accomplishment. It doesn't matter if we're trying to learn to make a good pasta sauce or master a new computer software program.

We typically discipline ourselves to lose an extra five, ten, or twenty pounds. But then we celebrate by returning to our old habits and watching every pound return. Why? We failed to develop a positive action plan at which we could be *persistent*. Honestly, can you think of any skill or endeavor that is not improved by a persistent effort?

The simplicity is having a goal that's important enough to you that you'll persist in the effort needed. How will this make you healthier, you ask? A stagnant pool of water has no sparkle. We are brightest when we are moving toward something that matters to us. Making an effort once, even if successful, is good but less fulfilling than working steadily to improve.

I am sure that my mother didn't bake the best pies in town on her first attempt. In fact, when she married my father, I am told that she couldn't cook at all, never mind bake.

Dad, who had started training to be a chef, taught her the basics. The rest is history. Her pies became the consistently closest thing to perfection imaginable. I never expect to find a crust that is lighter, flakier, or more delicious than Mom's. Nor am I apt to ever taste fillings that are any fresher, juicier, or so carefully spiced to accentuate the natural flavors. She accomplished becoming the undisputed Best Cook in Town status through persistence.

When I hear someone moaning and groaning about their lack of talent or luck or skill, I know better. They just haven't tried hard enough or long enough.

Think of a tennis match. The pros launch these rocket-propelled ace serves right past their opponents. Do they do this every time? No, but consistently ace quality serves are surely their goal.

They practice their serve hundreds of times each week. They aren't trying to best the 99.9% of the population they could beat without practice. They are persistent so they can consistently be the very best they can be when they face a like-minded professional. The best athletes want to beat the best, fair and square, with their hard-earned skills.

There is great fulfillment and satisfaction for all of us in having persistence pay off with consistent quality. Someone can easily have better raw talent than we do in some area. However, you can zoom past them if you are persistent in the necessary work to improve, and they allow their skills to stagnate. The simple truth is based on simple facts. We succeed when we are willing to do what it takes... over and over again.

All that I am, or ever hope to be,
I owe to my angel mother.
-- Abraham Lincoln (1809 – 1865)
American statesman, lawyer,
16th President of the United States

Skill 20
Honesty Is Vital

> *In the end, mothers are always right.*
> *No one else tells the truth.*
> -- Randy Susan Meyers (1952 -)
> American author

I recall an early lesson from Mom in honesty. As usual, my younger brother and I had been at the local grocery store with Mom. Groceries and children were all snugly loaded in the car, and Mom headed us for home.

Meanwhile, sitting in the back seat, my brother pulled some sort of candy out of his pocket. I do not recall whether it was gum or Lifesavers that he'd secretly picked up at the checkout.

What I clearly remember is
Mom driving straight back to the store.

She then proceeded to march my brother back inside to return his ill-gotten treasure and make him apologize to the store manager. Yikes! Lesson learned.

Honesty comes first, regardless of consequences.

Being honest does not mean being nasty or impolite. Blunt garbage is neither warranted nor excused.

Mom was teaching us to never take anything that belongs to someone else. Period.

If we're lucky, we all learn that lesson early in life. And we all learn it in different ways.

I recall a young stepdaughter getting in trouble for taking an apple from someone's bowl of apples in a school refrigerator. She'd initially smirked and tossed it off as irrelevant, saying, "It's just an apple."

Through this experience, however, she learned that it was not *just* an apple. It was someone *else's* apple.

Honesty is a very expensive gift.
Don't expect it from cheap people.
-- Warren Buffett (1930 -)
American investor, business tycoon, and philanthropist

Skill 21
Follow Your Dreams

> *It takes a lot of courage*
> *to show your dreams to someone else.*
> -- Erma Bombeck (1927 – 1996)
> American humorist

We have all likely heard the quips about not waiting for your ship to come in if you never sent it out. Or that you've got to have a dream to have a dream come true.

Mom put it well when she'd say things like, "It's good to have dreams. That makes you try harder." So true.

When we have dreams, be they large or small by anyone's standards, we have a sense of purpose. Our dreams give us drive. Our dreams inspire us.

We do need to take care not to idly chase ideas. However, when we truly want to achieve something, we should focus our efforts on learning what we need to do to attain success.

We shouldn't spend all our time on learning, naturally. We humans may just sit comfortably in the learning mode, even for years.

Action is required, even though we may make mistakes along the way. We must do what needs to be done to make our dreams come true.

When we envision attaining our dream, we can set goals. It helps when we set little goals to help achieve our ultimate goal.

Reaching small levels of success helps stoke the fires. It gives us hope. It builds confidence that we really can get it done.

Having dreams and following our dreams also keeps our spirits young and free. As children, we easily dreamt big. Nothing was out of our reach.

Surprise. Welcome to adulthood. What now?

Nothing IS out of our reach.

Pursuing dreams can also make us more interesting people. This is a natural occurrence with people who keep themselves in the learning and growing mode. Besides, having a dream not only makes life feel more worthwhile. Dreams are fun!

Go for it!

Hold fast to dreams for if dreams die,
life is a broken winged bird that cannot fly.
-- Langston Hughes (1902 – 1967)
American poet

Skill 22
Avoid Being Fickle

> *Our criteria for deciding what's good*
> *and what's bad is very fickle,*
> *especially in this country.*
> -- Roberta Flack (1937 -)
> American singer

Being fickle is defined as changing frequently, especially with regard to one's loyalties, interests, and affections. We likely know or have known many people who aptly fit the definition.

Sometimes people drive us crazy because their temperaments are so different than our own. Sometimes they give us pause because they keep us off balance. People who are fickle are the ones who keep us off balance.

They vehemently tell us of some decision they have made. Within days or even hours they are behaving or stating something in exact opposition to what they'd sworn.

Often a person who is fickle behaves with great outward confidence. They seem very sure-footed and sure-minded. We can be slow to understand that theirs is a false bravado. When someone is insecure or suffering from low self-esteem, they can change their minds frequently about any number of things. They often have a fear of failure.

Being fickle delivers a flexibility that helps them keep their options open. However, their lack of true decisiveness makes life very unstable for those closest to them.

Someone announces their decision. You make your plans and schedule and actions to accommodate that decision. Suddenly, they announce an opposite decision. You change your plans and schedule and re-do the actions taken to accommodate the reversal in decision. Then, lo and behold, they change their minds yet again.

The good living skill taught by Mom in this regard was clear. She taught us to make a solid decision. She stressed that we then had to live with the outcome of that decision.

She was teaching us responsibility. She was teaching us to make better decisions in the future.

Learning to make good decisions and take responsibility for their repercussions is part of our maturation.

Many people grow up without this skill. These tend to be people who have advanced in years, but not in maturity.

Good decision making takes into account the impact of their decisions on those around them.

No one wants to become known as someone who repeatedly makes others jump through hoops. Worse yet, we don't want to be known as someone who then makes those same people jump backward through the hoops, and then, perhaps, reversing themselves again.

Muhammed Ali Jinnah, the founder of Pakistan, is noted for saying, "I do not believe in making the right decision. I take a decision and make it right."

In business, I was taught a spin on that. And I like the responsibility factor that it adds.

Make a decision, make it yours, make it right.

By making a decision our own, we take away our ability to blame circumstances or someone else. We are claiming our decision as our own. Then we can set about making it right. We make the decision make sense and follow it through. If it turns out to have been a poor decision, the responsibility is fully our own to apologize, make corrections and changes, and move forward. We must not allow ourselves to become fickle out of fear of failure or anything else.

Of mankind, we may say in general they are fickle, hypocritical, and greedy of gain.
-- Niccolo Machiavelli (1469 – 1527)
Italian Renaissance diplomat, philosopher & writer

Skill 23
Take Responsibility

When you are arguing with a fool,
make sure he isn't doing the same thing.
-- Unknown

We love having rights, but we often fail to recognize that rights come with responsibilities. Ah, there it is... the dreaded "R" word. Responsibility.

Life is much easier when we can look at what is happening through lenses that make negative more comfortable. None of us likes thinking of ourselves as playing a role in our own negativity, never mind having full responsibility for our reactions or responses to it.

Mom's lesson here was simple. When we make a mistake, it is our own. Stop looking for someone else or some circumstance to blame.

Yuk. But she was right. We each choose our attitudes, words, and actions. We only look weak when we try to cast blame on others.

We all know people who do this. We are not impressed. Their lack of responsibility becomes a highly annoying habit. That is one habit we do not want to emulate.

These are the folks who seem to think they can do no wrong. If they overreact to something, it's always justified. Well, it's justified in their mind. In truth there is nothing someone can do or say that gives us true cause to rationalize how we respond.

We each make a personal choice as to how we respond each and every time.

When we make a mistake, Mom taught us to correct it if we can. If we can't, then we should apologize sincerely.

We should also use our errors to learn to behave better the next time. This means we learn not to repeat the negative action. Then we should turn the page. Let it go. It can be difficult, but we must learn not to beat ourselves up repeatedly.

Look at the word responsibility – "response" – "ability" – the ability to choose your response.
-- Stephen Covey (1932 – 2012)
American educator, businessman & author

Skill 24
Learn from Mistakes

There will be so many times you feel like you failed.
But in the eyes, heart, and mind of your child
you are super mom.
-- Stephanie Precourt
American blogger & writer

The best experience to learn from is that of others, but we humans are stubborn. We can be told the stove is hot, but, inevitably, we reach out to try to touch it for verification. This is how we learn. We learn from our mistakes.

We must make many mistakes ourselves. Sometimes often. In my stepmother shoes, I tried to encourage the young ones to try to avoid the truly serious mistakes. You know, the ones that have long-term or even deadly repercussions.

My mother always encouraged us to find the lessons in each mistake. Not that young folks want to do a lot of analysis, but we understood her point. If we found the lesson or lessons we learned from each mistake, we might not need to *repeat* that mistake.

When we make bad choices and decisions, we have options. We can look for someone else to blame. We can recognize our responsibility in our actions.

Making mistakes and learning from them helps us build wisdom. When we gain and use wisdom, we are developing good judgment, too.

Mom might ask us to write down what we think went wrong, what we could have done better, and even what we learned from the experience. This proved to be a valuable good living skill as an adult, because it also developed and exercised our analytical abilities. Best of all? We can keep growing and learning from our mistakes for our entire lives. Typically, the mistakes become less frequent and more minor. These are good things!

Success is the ability to go from failure to failure without losing your enthusiasm.
-- Sir Winston Spencer Churchill (1874 – 1965)
British politician and Prime Minster of the United Kingdom

Skill 25
Hold Your Head High

Keep your head up.
God gives his hardest battles to his strongest soldiers.
-- Unknown

This is not prideful. This is survival. Not allowing rejection to define us is a learned skill. We are not born with it.

When something doesn't go exactly as planned, try to remember that YOU did not fail. Someone else simply didn't see your value... this time.

If you struggled socially through those awkward pre-teen years, you may relate to this next example. One day during 7th grade, a classmate and friend since kindergarten was talking about the pool party he would be hosting at his grandmother's house. He suddenly realized that I was sitting at the table among his invited guests.

My friend quipped, "You didn't get invited to my pool party because who'd want to see you in a bathing suit?"

Nice. Open rejection. Okay. I was the classic late bloomer. These are not the things that torment us as adults, but it's tough in junior high school. I laughed it off... naturally.

Then came high school. I was still lagging behind. I was not ready for prime time.

Walk on, Mom taught us. Stay busy. Hold your head high.

So, as a freshman I tried out for cheerleading and was named the junior varsity alternate. Well, I wasn't cute. I wasn't pretty. I was gawky and skinny. Even when one regular cheerleader was unable to cheer, I was never asked to fill in for her. Not once. Rejection. I found myself just wishing folks would accept me, "claim" me, maybe even like me.

Walk on. Stay busy. Hold your head high.

I did just that. I got involved in every club, sport, and activity possible. I learned to use my brains and my wits. My high school resume looked like a Who's Who template. By my senior year, the ugly duckling was emerging as a swan of sorts. I ended up the varsity cheerleading captain and represented my state in Mobile, Alabama at the America's Junior Miss Pageant.

Through the pits and the peaks, Mom was a constant. Mothers do that like no one else can. We are always perfectly fantabulous in their eyes, hearts, and minds.

I am so grateful for this good living skill. Hold your head high.

Never bend your head. Always hold it high.
Look the world straight in the eye.
-- Helen Keller (1880 – 1968)
American author and political activist

Skill 26
No Idle Hands

Well done is better than well said.
-- Unknown

Some good living skills are taught through words. Some are taught through examples. Most are taught with a combination. Those who teach us are best when they walk the walk, rather than just talking the talk.

Blessedly, Mom was that kind of teacher. We'd hear her say the words.

"Work for it."

"Everyone works here."

"A little work never hurt anyone."

And she did those things. She worked hard.

She taught us that no one owed us anything in this world. We needed to work hard for it, constantly.

Nothing worth having would be simply handed to us. It was up to us to earn it.

As you can well imagine, Mom was not the only one who did chores at home. Dad orchestrated outdoor chores, and Mom orchestrated indoor chores. We all took part. It was expected. We were not paid an allowance. These were our family duties.

Well, my little brother started displaying his knack for business at a very young age. He was too little to do regular chores. However, he was put in charge of emptying small wastebaskets into the big kitchen wastebasket. For the first time in our family, he was offered a financial incentive. He would be paid 5 cents for emptying the wastebasket.

Okay, he got a little carried away. If someone had dropped one tissue in the bathroom wastebasket, he promptly carried it to the kitchen to empty. Then asked for his nickel. Clever.

We were all to take part in sharing duties and chores. We learned that we should always be doing something worthwhile.

We were taught to keep busy. This meant we should keep busy doing something productive.

Television watching time was strictly limited. There would be no lying around doing nothing in our home. No one did that. No one was bored. Everyone kept busy.

Mom lived this example. If she was sitting down, she was probably writing a thank you note to someone... or preparing a grocery list... or planning dinner... or ironing that day's wash.

Even when we, as a family, were in the car, she stayed busy, when not driving, of course. I can recall many times when Dad was driving that Mom would be busily working beside him.

She might have been doing some mending. Or perhaps snapping fresh green beans from our garden in preparation for dinner. She was always busy. Her good living skill lesson has always stayed with me. I practice this to this day… no idle hands.

***If evolution really works,
how come mothers only have two hands?***
-- Milton Berle (1908 – 2002)
American comedian & actor

Skill 27
Work to Be Independent

I want my children
to have all the things I couldn't afford.
Then, I want to move in with them.
-- Phyllis Diller (1917 – 2012)
American actress & comedienne

This means more than learning to cook and sew, garden and build, earn money and take care of responsibilities. It means learning to be self-reliant, discovering our abilities, and trusting ourselves.

The first lesson I recall in this endeavor was frustrating. I didn't know how to spell a word, so I'd ask.

Mom's answer was always the same. "Look it up."

Argh! If I could look it up, I would already know how to spell the word! Nope. She meant to figure it out. Look it up several times if need be.

It worked. I ended up becoming a regular success at Spelling Bees. Of course, this was before computers and the Internet and our ability to "Google" anything.

Because information is now so readily and instantly available, I fear that children today don't get the advantage of learning to persist in the discovery of knowledge. I hope that "ease" in thinking does not overflow into "entitlement" attitudes that hold them back from seeking and developing as much independence as possible.

I have yet to hear a man ask for advice on how to combine marriage and a career.
-- Gloria Steinem (1934 -)
American feminist and social activist

Of course, Mom also championed us having time to play. As kids, our folks encouraged plenty of play time. I think that is natural. First, we play in Life. Then we enter our more serious learning and formal education years.

Then we take that knowledge and those learned skills and apply them in our working lives to sustain and build and develop our independence.

Ultimately, we can slow down and start to enjoy the fruits of our labor in our retirement years. This phase is more for reflection on those good living lessons that we learned.

I also love when people who have grown and succeeded share their wisdom with others. Wisdom shared doesn't remove the necessitation of young people learning to work hard to earn their own independence. But wisdom can deliver some worthy shortcuts, when we are open to learning.

Work is either fun or drudgery.
It depends on your attitude. I like fun.
-- Colleen C. Barrett (1944 -)
President Emeritus of Southwest Airlines
(1st woman to serve as president of a major airline)

Skill 28
Rise Above the Fray

My mother is a walking miracle.
-- Leonardo DiCaprio (1974 -)
American actor & film producer

Moms are wonderful when it comes to helping us not sink into crabbiness or negativity. My mom's living example of positivity is legendary. This always included the importance of not judging others.

Mom taught us to never judge someone based on the opinion of others. Not only should we not speak ill of other people, but we should take with a grain of salt all negative spewed about them by other people.

This is so true. Even when we may think we have all the facts we should still not sit in judgment. Hello! That's God's place.

Rising above the fray becomes increasingly difficult lately. Any time we turn on the television or radio or even venture online, we get a constant bombardment of negativity.

Someone important may do something wonderful. Someone may say something extremely positive about an important person's character or actions. These things rarely make the news.

I understand. As a journalist, I remember living in a constant battle to report what was happening, rather than just focusing on negativity. Sadly, the "if it bleeds, it leads" thinking tends to dominate. This has more to do with human nature than anything else.

Media outlets must maintain good ratings to stay viable. Though we may cry out for more good news, we humans tend to be more drawn to negative than positive news. So much of today's news harps on repeating someone's bitterly partisan and negative analysis of someone else. We can and must do better than this.

Far too many influential people seem utterly focused on "flushing" anyone whose opinions differ. Yikes! A "cancel culture" is FAR from free, never mind being the opposite of progressive or open-minded.

Should you ever find yourself the victim of other people's bitterness, smallness, or insecurities, remember things could be worse... You could be *them*.

Grateful barely begins to describe how I feel about having been taught to not judge a book by its cover. We've all heard that beauty may only be skin deep. But Mom taught me to look for quality in people, rather than physical appearance. She was right, naturally. It is in a person's heart, soul, and spirit that true beauty shines.

In teaching us to rise above the fray, we also learned to both be and seek people with inner beauty and depth of character. We learned not to take part in belly-aching or spewing negativity about someone else.

When you challenge
other people's ideas of who or how you should be,
they may try to diminish and disgrace you.
It can happen in small ways, in hidden places,
or in big ways on a world stage.
You can spend a lifetime resenting the tests, angry
about the slights and the injustices.
Or, you can rise above it.
-- Carly Fiorina (1954 -)
American businesswoman & political figure

Skill 29
If You Are in the Fight, Fight to Win

> *My mom is my hero.*
> *[She] inspired me to dream when I was a kid.*
> *Anytime anyone inspires you to dream,*
> *that's gotta be your hero.*
> -- Tim McGraw (1967 -)
> American singer, actor, record producer

Mom's good living skill lesson here was to not sit on Life's sidelines and watch. Become as active as we possibly could be.

We must learn to not let life simply happen to us or around us. We can and should make things happen on purpose.

Professional athletes don't become superstars by performing in an average or hap-hazard fashion. They work hard. They practice for years. They train deliberately. They pour on their very best performance, again and again.

The same is true in Life as in sports… We need to be in it to win it.

If we hesitate when we should act, we are waiting for others to take control. That is rarely anyone's true goal. We want to get and stay in control of our own destiny.

This starts with our intent. Our intent must be followed by our actions. This is how we win.

Often the sacrifices involved in attaining our victories, come in the form of missed immediate gratification. We pass by the little rewards to continue striving for the big picture.

Inevitably, once we have made the decision to fight for something, we also must decide that we will fight to win. This requires hard work. Hard work is often followed by even harder work.

The fight is won or lost away from witnesses – behind the lines, in the gym, and out there on the road, long before I dance under those lights.
-- Muhammad Ali (1942 – 2016)
American professional boxer

Skill 30
Stay Open-Minded

An angry man opens his mouth and shuts up his eyes.
-- Cato (234 BC – 149 BC)
Roman soldier, senator, & historian

Shouting or repeating a position, opinion, or stand does not add validity or weight or worth. To begin with, that position should be true. Neither repetition nor volume can make it true. That said, both repetition and volume tend to make a great many people *believe* what is said. Sadly, they often become convinced of something that wasn't even true. It was just somebody's wish, whim, or spin.

In politics, we can be driven crazy by all the ranting and raving against someone or some idea. High volume does not equate with fact. Hello!

In fact, I have come to learn that if someone must shriek their position or constantly repeat it, they are trying to convince me, not educate me or anyone else.

They are trying to convince by pressure, by appearing as if "most people" agree with them. By stating something over and over it must make it somehow true. Right? Nope.

Mom taught me to stay open-minded because many people may have many different opinions. Some of those opinions will make no sense to us. Some may be wonderful. Regardless, we are all better when we sincerely listen to others.

Further, she taught that we are all better when we encourage people to feel or believe differently than we do. It does not make them *less*. It makes us *more*.

Listening to others is the right thing to do, even when they don't know enough to do the same.

We never know when some piece of information may come forward that shapes, strengthens, or even changes our opinions or thoughts. So, we always need to listen.

This is powerful in helping us stay in the growth and learning mode throughout our lives.

Always remember, however, that we do not have to change our opinions to please our friends. It's perfectly all right to have friends with dramatically juxtaposed opinions, even politically.

We all know folks in front of whom we don't bother to mention anything political. They have their ideas and don't want to even hear anything that differs. That's fine. Don't try to enlighten someone who doesn't want illumination. That would be akin to trying to teach a pig to sing, or pushing a rope, or putting the toothpaste back into the tube. It would be just plain frustrating.

However, opinions are often shared just like advice, but truth is often not heard. The truth cannot be heard when the other person will not listen. So, we need to stay open-minded and listen. That does *not* mean we must change our beliefs.

Someone says, "You don't listen to me."

What they may mean is that we don't **do** as **they** would have us do. There is a belief held by many that if we listen to them, we would understand that their way or their opinion is better than ours. We should change to mirror their wishes and thoughts. That is simply not true.

We can listen with an open mind, but we need not change to reflect someone else's wishes. Mom knew what she was talking about when she told me that we can't possibly please everyone, and it would be frustratingly impossible to try.

So, we always need to listen with an open mind. Then we can process the information for ourselves. Ultimately, we should follow our own heart. Do what we believe is right.

> *It takes two to speak the truth —*
> *one to speak and another to hear.*
> -- Henry David Thoreau (1817 – 1862)
> American essayist & philosopher

Skill 31
Find the Humor in "Don'ts"

She raised us with humor,
and she raised us to understand that not everything was
going to be great— but how to laugh through it.
-- Liza Minnelli (1946 -)
American actress, singer & dancer
(speaking about her mother, Judy Garland)

The good living skill learned from Mom here is to recognize and accept ourselves as mere humans. Most importantly? Keep a sense of humor about it all.

Whether we intend to or not, we are all susceptible to speaking words that sound logical in some way or another. However, on second glance, we see some level of silliness.

This reminds me of the words Jason Kidd spoke upon being drafted to the Dallas Mavericks. Kidd proudly announced, "We're going to turn this team around 360 degrees." Okay. That puts us right back where we started.

Be them funny or not, parents tend to use some common rants. Most of us have heard a plethora of instructions that come in the form of common parental sayings. They may be the "Do as I say, not as I do" sort.

Or perhaps you've heard (or delivered) the effervescent response to the child's whining question, "Whyyyyyy?" That answer, of course, being, "Because I said so."

Mom used to wince as I'd sing along with Louis Armstrong on the radio. Oh, yes, I always gave it my best vocal growl to mimic his. I love Satchmo! Decades later I still break out my growl to sing along with him on the radio.

Well, Mom wasn't overly impressed. She would regularly respond with her loving scolding.

"Don't do that," she'd implore. "Your voice might stay like that."

We've likely heard, "Don't make those faces. Your face could get stuck like that."

Me, too. I still like making funny faces. And, no. Neither my face nor voice ever got stuck in any one of them.

· With a good sense of humor, we learn to look back on these many phrases and smile. Although I do recall my sister and I, as children, often quipping that if we ever had children, we would never say…. This or that… any number of these standard lines that annoyed us as kids.

Then as adults, I heard my sister using one of the lines on her daughter. I quietly reminded her that we'd promised to never say such things if we had kids.

"Ohhhhh!" My sister wailed. "You are right!"

It's not easy being a Mother.
If it were, Fathers would do it.
-- Unknown

No, I am not trying to put down fathers. I had a fabulous father, too. I am merely reflecting on and celebrating Mom.

Meanwhile, we are all just humans. We all try to do our very best.

And it's sometimes fun to look at our commonality. We heard the expressions. We grow up and use the expressions.

"Don't cry over nothing; I'll give you something to cry about."

"If you don't eat your dinner now while it's hot, I'll let you eat it cold for breakfast."

"Don't pout with that lower lip stuck out, or I'll put a teacup on it."

And, of course, the classic we already mentioned. "I don't have to explain why. It's because I said so, that's why."

So, we learn to embrace the vital good living skill of keeping our sense of humor. Laughter always helps us keep perspective. A mother's work is rewarding, but only after she has survived mountains of frustration that we kids have inspired.

Everybody wants to save the Earth;
nobody wants to help Mom do the dishes.
-- P.J. O'Rourke (1947 -)
American political satirist

Skill 32
Get Back Up

My mother was the most beautiful woman I ever saw.
All I am I owe to my mother.
I attribute my success in life to the moral, intellectual
and physical education I received from her.
-- George Washington (1732 – 1799)
American military general; 1st President of the United States

We all fall down. What makes us strong is getting back up again.

Mom was a powerful advocate of getting back up and trying again. And again. And again. She helped make us stronger, healthier people by learning to persist despite the odds or setbacks. She would never even consider suggesting we give up. She'd say, "That's okay. You'll do better next time."

That was the presumption. We would try again. There would be a next time. And she encouraged us to go for it. Try again.

Whoever said anybody has a right to give up?
-- Marian Wright Edelman (1939 -)
American children's rights activist

We mustn't let our mistakes define who we are. Failures are a part of every life. If we allow ourselves to give up and not try again, we are supporting discouragement. We are crushing our own spirits.

Even when we don't feel like it, we must learn to be our own Encouragers. These are vital skills. Mom knew it. She never permitted us to suffer through pity parties. No way.

In hindsight, I recognize that, as children, most of us are blessed to not know extreme hardship. This is not to say many of us have not had to learn to endure and overcome. Quite the contrary. I mean, we may have lost a parent or sibling at a very young age. We may have been raised in a single parent household. We may have been raised without the benefit of financial security.

While there are a great many common challenges for children, most of us enjoyed a very blessed childhood. We were not raised in a rodent- or insect-infested space. We were not living with a dirt floor.

We did not fear people with guns blasting through our doors at any moment on every single night. We did not live in the middle of a war zone nor become accustomed to hearing bombs on a nightly basis. We did not have to endure squalid conditions with people dying in horrible ways all around us.

Still, we need to learn to strengthen our convictions. We need to learn to endure. We need to learn to persevere.

Resiliency can be learned, but we only learn to bounce back when we are assured that making a mistake is perfectly all right. In a healthy atmosphere, we are encouraged to try and try again, despite the inevitable mistakes we will make.

This teaches us to dare to get back up again and again. Our spirits are strengthened by the good living skills we have learned.

Thank you yet again and again, Mom.

Mothers are like glue.
Even when you can't see them,
they're still holding the family together.
-- Susan Gale
American educator

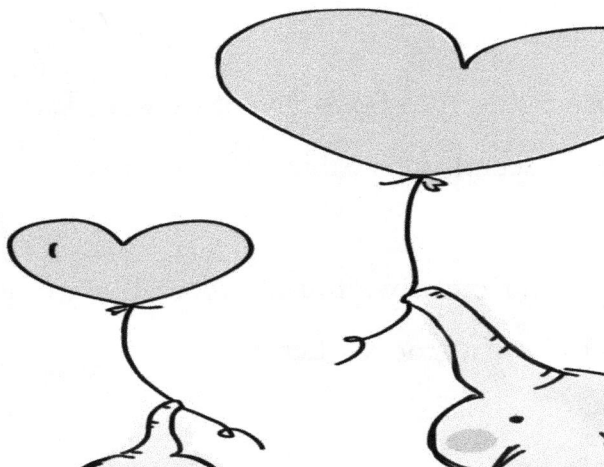

Skill 33
<u>Forgive</u>

A mom forgives us all our faults,
not to mention one or two we don't even have.
-- Robert Brault
American free-lance writer

Mom is the miraculous forgiver. No matter how many times we children may have disappointed her or even wounded her heart, she forgave us. She loved us. She taught us to do the same.

Because we need to be forgiven, we must learn to forgive, even when it seems impossible. No one is perfect. No one.

This doesn't mean we must forget. But we do not need nor want to hold a grudge. Let it go.

When we say that we've turned the page, we need to understand what that means. It means we are not going to look backward. We are not going to take the hurt that was done to us and throw it in the perpetrator's face at some later time. We have not forgotten. We likely will protect ourselves in the future. But we have turned the page. We have let it go.

This also helps us to not distrust others because of something bad done to us by someone else. Too often we find someone who totally distrusts people who have done absolutely nothing to earn the distrust. Someone else caused an individual great pain, so much so that they let themselves believe that everyone else would do the same.

This is sad. This is beyond sad. We live happier, fuller lives when we dare to trust.

Good people can do bad things,
and bad people can do good things.
-- Max DePree (1924 – 2017)
American businessman

Without forgiveness, there can be no real freedom to act. Without forgiveness we simply wander through a dark life with a misguided belief that someone... or *every*one... is out to get us or do us harm.

There are plenty of negative people out there. There are plenty of untrustworthy ones also. While we want to be careful, we also want to take care to not presume the worst in people.

Most people will treat us right.
We should focus on the people who do so.

This brings to mind a great tale shared via the Internet some years ago. It is called the Law of the Garbage Truck. Here it is.

The Law of the Garbage Truck

One day I hopped in a taxi and we took off for the airport. We were driving in the right lane when suddenly a black car jumped out of a parking space right in front of us. My taxi driver slammed on his brakes, skidded, and missed the other car by just inches! The driver of the other car whipped his head around and started yelling at us. My taxi driver just smiled and waved at the guy. And I mean, he was really friendly.

So, I asked, "Why did you just do that? This guy almost ruined your car and sent us to the hospital!"

This is when my taxi driver taught me what I now call, "The Law of the Garbage Truck." He explained that many people are like garbage trucks. They run around full of garbage, full of frustration, full of anger, and full of disappointment. As their garbage piles up, they need a place to dump it, and sometimes they'll dump it on you. Don't take it personally.

Just smile, wave, wish them well, and move on. Don't take their garbage and spread it to other people at work, at home, or on the streets.

The bottom line is that successful people do not let garbage trucks take over their day. Life's too short to wake up in the morning with regrets, so..... "Love the people who treat you right. Pray for the ones who don't."

If we practice an eye for an eye and a tooth for a tooth, soon the whole world will be blind and toothless.
-- Mahatma Gandhi (1869 – 1948)
Indian lawyer and political ethicist

FORGIVENESS

Skill 34
Keep the Faith

God could not be everywhere,
and, therefore, he made mothers.
-- Rudyard Kipling (1865 – 1936)
English journalist, writer & novelist

Among the many good living skills that I learned from my mother is the importance of faith. When we believe in something far greater than ourselves, we are strengthened by our humbleness.

Our faith shines light into the darkest corners. In our times of the greatest doubt or fear or trouble, our faith lifts us up and delivers hope.

Sometimes we feel too weak to get back up, too powerless to make a difference, too small to matter. Faith builds our strength, deepens our convictions, and boosts our abilities by teaching us about purpose.

Martin Luther King once said, "Faith is taking the first step even when you don't see the whole staircase." I like that. It reminds me that faith requires belief in something that science may not be able to prove. It requires faith in something we cannot see directly. But it also helps us to live better lives.

We learned early on to keep the Lord, Sunday school, and Church central in our lives. This includes the Golden Rule to treat others as we want to be treated, even when (perhaps especially when) they are not treating others well.

Throughout our lives we see far too many examples of man's inhumanity to man. Horrendous acts seem inexplicable. They can drain our strength and our faith, if we let them.

This is one reason I believe it is important to regularly renew our faith. When we stay in communication with the Lord, we stay stronger than when we distance ourselves.

In some of the toughest times, when we truly struggle to understand, it helps to remind ourselves that despite our free will, it I not all up to us. God is in control.

Our faith helps us through a wide variety of stressful times. Our faith shines the light at the end of the darkest tunnels. Our faith teaches us both humility and patience.

If you believe that we humans were made to thrive, not just survive, then keep the faith. In the toughest times in our families, personal or professional lives, or even our societies, don't give up on people who seem the most confused.

Often, the most negative people are also the weariest and the most lost. When we let our faith shine through us, we can be the humble servant who helps them find their way home.

And who knows? Perhaps our faith can encourage others to stand strong.

When we tell others that we're keeping them in our prayers, we need to be sure we are doing so. We must follow through and keep doing the very best that we can to keep the faith.

Faith is to believe what you do not see.
The reward of this faith is to see what you believe.
-- Saint Augustine (Aurelius Augustinus Hipponensis)
(354 – 430AD)
Roman African theologian & philosopher

Skill 35
Marriage Is Wonderful, Though Not Easy

It's not what we have in life,
but who we have in our life that matters.
-- Unknown

Life always brings challenges. However, trusting in your best friend and spouse helps us survive the bumps in the road.

With the legal bond of marriage comes the fact that simply walking away in tough times becomes more challenging. If love and faith aren't strong enough to see us through a storm with some clarity and steadfastness, then perhaps legal complications can help.

He rules the roost. She rules the rooster.

That quips lightly about how a husband and wife work out living together. Each couple figures it out to be successful.

A good line I have often seen has been said by many, though I know not who may have originally said or written it first. "A perfect marriage is just two imperfect people who refuse to give up on each other." That reflects the awareness of lifetime companions who are truly best friends.

My Mom and Dad were together for some 70 years. Yes, and still speaking! Still very much in love.

We lost my Dad a couple of years ago, following a very courageous battle with a third cancer. He struggled mightily in the hospital from the effects of anesthesia following a difficult surgery. He was slipping away. I sat with my Mother, as we talked about the fact that he seemed to have given up.

Mom quietly said, "I just thought we'd have a little more time."

Okay. How can anyone ever truly be ready to say good-bye to their best friend and soul mate of 70+ years?

So, we worked out a plan. I would focus on working his muscles and his spirit *for* him and doing everything we could to bring him back into fighting mode. Considering his condition, he would have to join this fight at some point. That was our plan's goal.

We worked diligently each day in the hospital.... Exercising his fingers, toes, arms and legs... offering positive words and enthusiastic encouragement... monitoring the medical activities and helping in every way we could.

The other part of the plan was keeping Mom healthy through it all. Her stress level was understandably high. I was honored to be able to be with her to try to help ease her load, to drive her the hour to and the hour from the hospital each day, and to be sure she was having the best chances to rest, eat, and sleep.

Our prayers were answered. Dad made it through his recovery. He got more time. *They* got more time.

Mom would never truly be "prepared" for the man she'd loved since she met him at age 16 to be gone, but she got more time with him.

Most of us have occasions when we don't think we can stand to even be in the same room with someone we love. They may have infuriated or frustrated us so badly.

It's far from easy to stand by someone who seems to have little or no regard or respect for us, never mind love or caring.

Whether or not we grew up in a home with loving parent types who could teach us by good examples, we can learn from relationships that do shine.

Did my folks drive each other crazy from time to time? Naturally. Their love and mutual respect helped see them through any darkness.

I try daily to learn from their example. Sometimes I succeed. Sometimes I need to improve.

Many things that are wonderful in this world, from relationships and education to sports and careers, are not easy. That does not mean they are not worthwhile.

Relationships can be very aggravating at times. Even little things can start to irk us.

One partner squeezes the toothpaste tube neatly from the bottom. The other squeezes it firmly in the middle. If we can stop being irked long enough, we can simply smile at the person who we love. Together we can find a solution. Sometimes it's as simple as buying a second tube of toothpaste.

Mom and Dad both taught me that teamwork is working together, even when apart. Teamwork doesn't tolerate the inconvenience of distance... especially in this age of technology.

When the going gets tough, I try to remember this good living reality. Marriage is wonderful, though not easy.

The essence of marriage is companionship,
and the woman you face across the coffee urn
every morning for ninety-nine years
must be both able to appreciate your jokes
and sympathize with your aspirations.
-- Elbert Hubbard (1856 – 1915)
American writer, publisher & philosopher

Skill 36
Love with All Your Heart

> *Mother's love is peace.*
> *It need not be acquired, it need not be deserved.*
> -- Erich Fromm (1900 – 1980)
> German psychologist, sociologist & philosopher

I can't count the many conversations with Mom in which she heartfully shares a story as tears are choking her words. It may be about something that has happened or some friend she spoke with earlier.

The topic matters less than the beautiful fact that she feels herself living. She courageously lets it show. It's just one more beautiful example she has always set for us.

Things may not always go our way. Our hearts may be broken. But if we give it our all, we need have no regrets.

It takes great courage to love fully, to love with all our heart. We are putting ourselves on the line with full exposure.

We need great faith and trust to do this. But it's worthwhile, if we dare.

We actually can *love* someone, even when we do not *like* their actions. We can still keep them in our heart.

In fact, when someone is troubled or troubling, they need even more love. This can be difficult when they say things or do things that are hurtful. Remember, it's actually okay to not like someone we love.

They may not choose to behave in a manner that helps us like them. However, when we love unconditionally, we love. That is learning to love as a mother loves.

Someone's unlikable actions may break our hearts. Only we decide if we will cancel our love.

All women become like their mothers.
That is their tragedy.
No man does. That's his.
-- Oscar Wilde (1854 – 1900)
Irish poet & playwright

Skill 37
Choose to Be a Positive Role Model

I would say that my mother
is the single biggest role model in my life,
but that term doesn't seem to encompass enough
when I use it about her.
She was the love of my life.
-- Mindy Kaling (1979 -)
American actress & comedienne

Whenever I spoke with students, which for much of my career happened quite frequently, being a role model arose as a common theme. I found myself reflecting one of those vital good living skills I'd learned from Mom.

We are all role models to someone else. Someone is always watching us. We matter to someone... whether we know it or not, whether we like it or not, and whether we choose it or not.

What we do and say matters to someone. Mom taught by both her words and by the examples she set.

We are all role models.
Our only choice is to be a good or bad one.

Just imagine how wonderful it would be if everyone took that responsibility seriously. Children growing up would emulate positive images. They wouldn't worry about being short or tall, sexy or not, athletic or geeky. Kids wouldn't grow up trying to be like some tough guy or bully. They'd want to succeed and be kind to others. They'd give and lead honest lives. They'd try hard and celebrate their successes and the successes of others.

Every time we encourage others to be their best, we are reminding them of their strengths. We are also reinforcing their bond with us. They know they can count on us to help them achieve their goals and become their best person.

Role models set examples by living their standards. This is a good reason that we can't afford to be negative. Someone very impressionable is watching.

My mother was my role model
before I even knew what that word was.
-- Lisa Leslie (1972 -)
American professional basketball player & coach

Mine too. Remember, when I first started buying shoes for work, they were 3½-inch pumps... because THAT is what a lady wore. That is what Mom wore. As a child playing dress-up, I'd scuffed around in her shoes plenty of times. As an adult, I had to own them... in every color, of course. More importantly, Mom taught me to be a lady. This was very important to her, and it became very important to me. These lessons have always served me well.

It is my responsibility to help others.
To be a positive example.
I want to be a role model for others,
to help others like me get a chance.
-- Rob Jeter (1969 -)
American college football coach

Skill 38
Celebrate Life

Motherhood is the exquisite inconvenience
of being another person's everything.
-- Unknown

We tend to move through life quickly. We forget to stop to smell the roses... or enjoy the autumn foliage... or just relish a cool drink of water at the side of the road. Imagine simply taking a break to listen to the sounds around you.

There is always something worth celebrating. We exude light and lift everyone's energy when we celebrate.

Mom helped me to learn that I needed to celebrate each and every little milestone. I may not yet have reached my ultimate goal regarding some project, but she was quick to point out that I'd learned a lot or grown a lot as part of the process. Thus, I'd already won.

So, milestones, or intermediary goals, or steps along the way... they are all worth recognizing. They are all worth celebrating.

I remember visiting the Tennis Hall of Fame in Newport, Rhode Island. I loved reading the quotes by various tennis greats of yesterday and today. One in particular stands out to me as important, especially today.

Top-ranked American tennis legend, Billie Jean King, who ranked number one in the world six times, exhibited great wisdom when she said, "It's just really important that we start celebrating our differences. Let's start tolerating first, but then we need to celebrate our differences."

As a gay rights activist, she was addressing sexuality. However, we can apply her words to politics, too.
I, for one, have had way more than enough of the name calling and negative labeling as people repeatedly try to slam or shame or "cancel" anyone.

Of course, they mean anyone who believes differently than they do. I am sick of political correctness and pressure to conform altogether.

Phooey! (If that's even still a word.)

Okay, I won't get into that rant here. I spoke my piece on that topic in my 2018 book, *The Bimbo Has MORE Brains... Surviving Political Correctness.*

I can't help but think, however, that we must become better at tolerating and understanding our differences. Then some magic could happen. Again, we could actually celebrate that thinking or believing differently is actually good and makes us all stronger.

In all aspects of life, we need checks and balances. It must never be about someone being right, so the other person must be wrong.

There is more than one right way
to do most things.

Sometimes we can be mightily lifted by simply *thinking* about a great concept worthy of celebrating. Think of it as positive thinking. That in itself can mark a milestone in our progress toward good living. Great concepts often evolve into more precious skills that all help make good living as easy as 1 – 2 – 3.

The more you praise and celebrate your life,
the more there is in life to celebrate.
-- Oprah Winfrey (1954 -)
American talk show host, actress & television producer

Skill 39
Make Every Moment Count

Every great dream begins with a dreamer.
Always remember, you have within you the strength,
the patience, and the passion
to reach for the stars to change the world.
-- Harriet Tubman (unknown – 1913)
American abolitionist

Life isn't like surfing. I have watched the surfer "dudes" and "dudettes" sitting atop their boards. They're just sitting there… or are they?

Nope. They're watching. They're counting. They're waiting for the perfect wave. When they see it coming, each one whips around, planting their bodies flat upon their boards, and paddling like crazy to get in synch with that oncoming perfect wave. They want to catch it just right.

To enjoy good living skills, life isn't quite the same. We need not wait for the perfect wave… the perfect moment. We need to take a moment and *make* it perfect.

Think of the famed Roman expression, "Carpe diem." There was no thought of waiting for tomorrow or some elusive perfect moment.

"Seize the day" resonates with many as an inspirational challenge to stop sitting on the fence and do something. Do it now. Do it right. But do it. Do not wait.

Mom would say, "Make the most of every moment." She offered no pity parties if things didn't go just the way we'd hoped.

For example, when I first auditioned for a part in a high school play, I failed to land a role. Hello. I was still expected to make every moment count. So, I'd build sets. I'd gather props. I'd sew costumes. I'd paint backdrops. I'd clean up the dressing room after everyone else had gone to the cast party. I'd make every moment count.

These were the experiences that taught me many other good living skills. One of the most precious is humility.

When my moment came to be on the stage acting, I quickly learned why tears ran down my face during curtain calls. Humility. I was taking a bow. I was getting a front row seat to the applause of the audience.

Yet, I fully knew I had not done it all by myself. I didn't deserve all that applause. Serving in the other roles, behind the scenes, had taught me how to make every moment count and to accept all appreciation received with great humility. I will never forget.

Our days on this planet Earth are incredibly few. When we are young, life seems to stretch on forever. We can't wait to grow up.

As adults, we tend to wish we could slow the ol' clock down a bit. Life flies by so very quickly.

We've heard them all.

- Don't count the days. Make the days count.

- If we waste our time, we waste our life.

- Regretting wasted time is wasting more time.

- Don't so focus on the finish line that we don't enjoy the journey.

- The things that count cannot be counted.

In truth, we all need to be reminded now and then about exactly how precious each day of our life is. We tend to get all rattled over all the stress from trying to get everything accomplished. It's as though we forget to breathe.

Stop. Breathe. Appreciate someone around you. We never know when we may be seeing someone for the last time. Make every moment count.

You are never too old
to set a new goal or dream a new dream.
-- C.S. Lewis (1898 – 1963)
British writer & theologian

Skill 40
Leave a Place Better Than You Found It

My Mother: She is beautiful, softened at the edges
and tempered with a spine of steel.
I want to grow old and be like her.
-- Jodi Picoult (1966 -)
American writer

Our family often rushed against the clock. We could be on time. We could be running late. It mattered little.

Mom would always clean up thoroughly as she headed out the door. At home, she fastidiously swept sand away from the door to help prevent our many shoes from tracking it into the house.

I will admit that I often caught her sweeping halfway down the driveway. Okay. Perhaps she carried it to an extreme. But perhaps not.

Her lesson was not lost on us to leave a place better than we found it. We often stayed in a little wooden cabin on Newfound Lake in Bristol, New Hampshire for a summer vacation.

After the car was packed to go home, and we kids were all sitting in the car, Mom would be sweeping out the cabin and sweeping off the entire porch. We were not going to leave a single grain of sand.

How often I have arrived at a place and found it dirty or otherwise unkept. I most assuredly would not dream of leaving it that way. Mom taught us well.

In Life, I try to apply this lesson on a wide variety of levels. Think about it.

What steps can we each take to leave our families, friends, communities, and even this planet better than when we found it?

This proves to be a powerful means of having a positive impact on our little spheres of influence. Everyone hopes to be a person who matters, even if to just one person. Or one situation. Or one business. Or one civic organization. Or one charitable cause.

If we take whatever steps we can to leave a place better than we found it, we make a powerful difference. We matter.

Thank you, Mom. Again and again and again. I deeply appreciate this and every lesson. And I will continue trying to pay all these good living skills forward, just the way you taught us.

So, here I go… again… in your honor… sweeping out the driveway.

Being a mother is learning about strengths you didn't know you had.
-- Linda Wooten
American author

Conclusion

I hope you have enjoyed this light and loving look at the deep love a mother gives each child. It is my hope that viewing that love through some of the many valuable lessons my mother taught me reminded you of your own experiences. We all benefit when we pause to reflect on the love that surrounds us.

Perhaps you have also been inspired to reach out to your own mother or some other person who shared and embodied important good living skills for you. Never hesitate. Let them know now.

If that special person is no longer with us, include them in your prayers. We can always say "thank you." I believe we should say "thank you" and "I love you" again and again. I have never heard anyone say they've grown tired of hearing such expressions.

When someone gives us their time, listens to our words, or touches our heart, we should remember it. We shine a great deal of light on the world with a simple "thank you."

Thank *you* for taking the time to read my special gift to my very special mother. I am mightily blessed. It was an honor to write this book for her for her 90th birthday celebration as a sincere salute to great Moms everywhere.

Mom, thank you again. I love you more.

About the Author

Cathy Burnham Martin's first published work was at age 6, when an early poem won a town library contest. That was back when her parents refused to let her have the then-popular Chatty Cathy doll, stating that one chatty Cathy in the house was more than enough. Though poetry took a back seat, she has driven her writing and blabbing proficiencies along a highly eclectic career path through recruiting college students, corporate communications for a telecommunications company, TV broadcasting as News Anchor with an ABC affiliate, station management for an award-winning PEG access station, and bank organizing as Investor Relations Officer and Senior Vice President of Marketing. An active board member and volunteer, she received Easter Seals' David P. Goodwin Lifetime Commitment Award.

This professional voiceover artist, humorist, corporate communications geek, musical actress, journalist, and dedicated foodie earned numerous awards in journalism and business. She has written, produced, and hosted groundbreaking documentaries, TV specials, and news reports, from the Moscow Superpower Summit and the opening of the Berlin Wall to New Hampshire's First-in-the-Nation Presidential Primaries.

A born storyteller and business speaker, Cathy is a member of the Actors Equity Association and a media coach. A 20-year Professional Member of the National Speakers Association, she continues speaking and coaching through SpeakEasy Corporate Communications.

Cathy Burnham Martin narrates her books as well as those of other authors. Audiobooks appear on such sites as Audible.com, iTunes, and Amazon. In addition to fiction and nonfiction books, Cathy writes articles for the GoodLiving123.com website.

Other Titles
From Cathy Burnham Martin

Encouragement: How to Be and Find the Best

The Bimbo Has Brains… and Other Freaky Facts

The Bimbo Has MORE Brains… Surviving Political Correctness

A Dangerous Book for Dogs: Train Your Humans

Dog Days in the Life of the Miles-Mannered Man

Healthy Thinking Habits: Seven Attitude Skills Simplified

Of the Same Blood: Your Eurasian Heritage

Sage, Thyme & Other Life Seasonings: Perspectives

Fifty Years of Fabulous Family Favorites (Volumes 1-3)

Champagne! Facts, Fizz, Food & Fun

Dockside Dining: Round One

Dockside Dining: A Second Helping

Dockside Dining: Back for Thirds

Cranberry Cooking

Lobacious Lobster

The Communication Coach:
Business Communication Tips from the Pros

**To see all books and audiobooks
from Cathy Burnham Martin
go to www.GoodLiving123.com**